1

"Live as if you were to die tomorrow. Learn as if you were to live forever."

– Mahatma Gandhi

2

"That which does not kill us makes us stronger."

— *Friedrich Nietzsche*

3

"Be who you are and say what you feel, because those who mind don't matter and those who matter don't mind."

– Bernard M. Baruch

4

"We must not allow other people's limited perceptions to define us."

— Virginia Satir

5

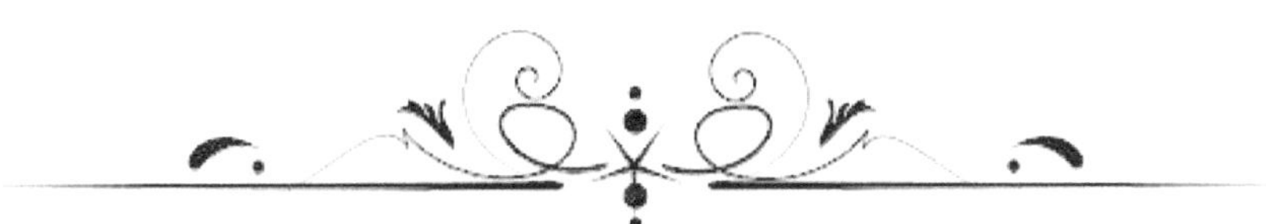

"Do what you can, with what you have, where you are."

– Theodore Roosevelt

6

"Be yourself; everyone else is already taken."

– Oscar Wilde

7

"This above all: to thine own self be true."

– *William Shakespeare*

8

"If you cannot do great things, do small things in a great way."

– Napoleon Hill

9

"If opportunity doesn't knock, build a door."

– Milton Berle

10

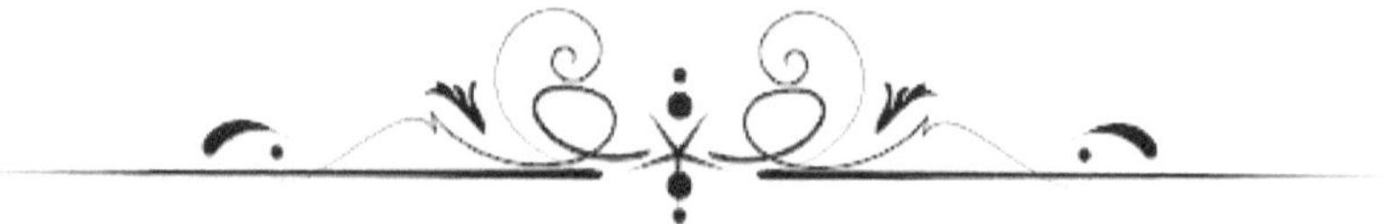

"Wise men speak because they have something to say; fools because they have to say something."

Plato

11

"Strive not to be a success, but rather to be of value."

– Albert Einstein

12

"Two roads diverged in a wood, and I—I took the one less traveled by, And that has made all the difference."

– Robert Frost

13

"Do not let what you cannot do interfere with what you can do."

– John Wooden

14

"Whenever you find yourself on the side of the majority, it is time to pause and reflect."

– Mark Twain

15

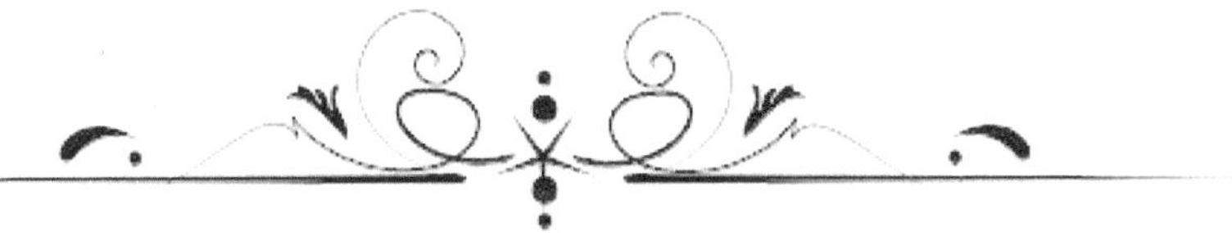

I haven't failed. I've just found 10,000 ways that won't work."

– Thomas Edison

16

"A journey of a thousand leagues begins beneath one's feet."

– *Lao Tzu*

17

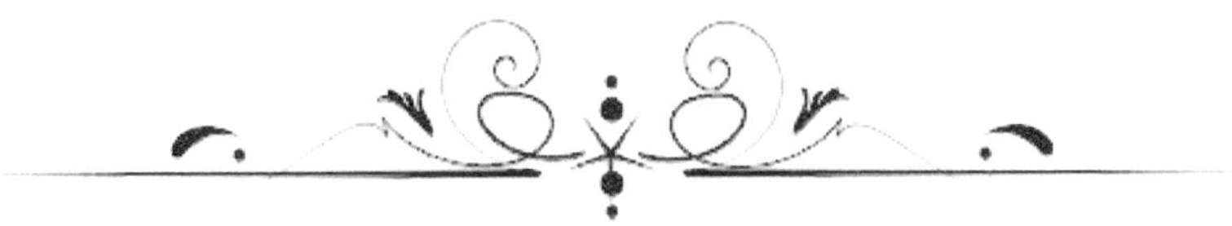

"I've learned that people will forget what you said, people will forget what you did, but people will never forget how you made them feel."

– Maya Angelou

18

"Either you run the day, or the day runs you."

— *Jim Rohn*

19

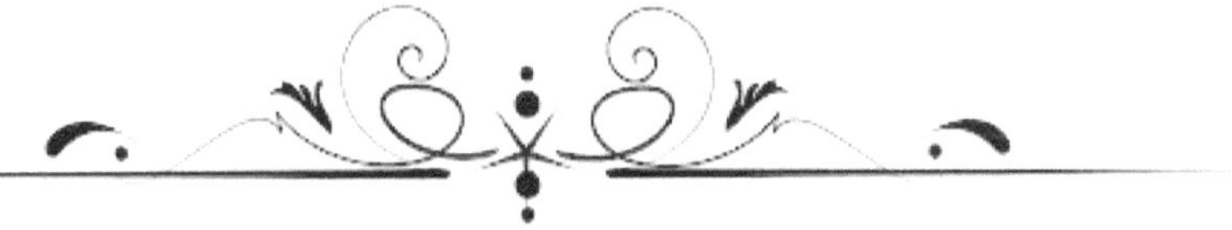

"You must be the change you wish to see in the world."

– Mahatma Gandhi

20

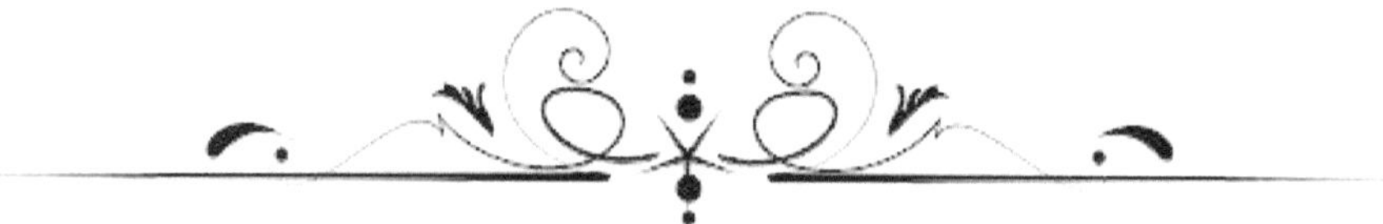

"What you do speaks so loudly that I cannot hear what you say."

— *Ralph Waldo Emerson*

21

"Believe and act as if it were impossible to fail."

– Charles Kettering

22

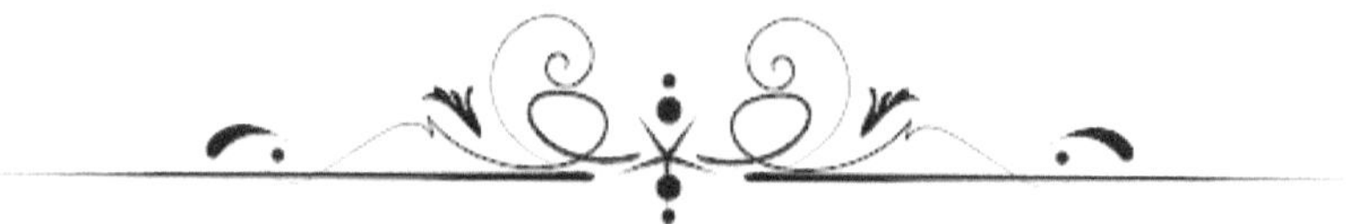

"The difference between ordinary and extraordinary is that little extra."

– Jimmy Johnson

23

"The best way to predict the future is to invent it."

– Alan Kay

24

"If I am not for myself, who is for me? And if I am only for myself, what am I? And if not now, when?"

– Rabbi Hillel

25

"Everything has beauty, but not everyone can see."

– *Confucius*

26

"Believe you can and you're halfway there."

– Theodore Roosevelt

27

"How wonderful it is that nobody need wait a single moment before starting to improve the world."

– Anne Frank

28

"Imagination is everything. It is the preview of life's coming attractions."

– Albert Einstein

29

"Change your thoughts and you change your world."

– Norman Vincent

30

"Happiness is not something ready made. It comes from your own actions."

– Dalai Lama

31

"Remember that happiness is a way of travel, not a destination."

– *Roy M. Goodman*

32

"Too many of us are not living our dreams because we are living our fears."

– Les Brown

33

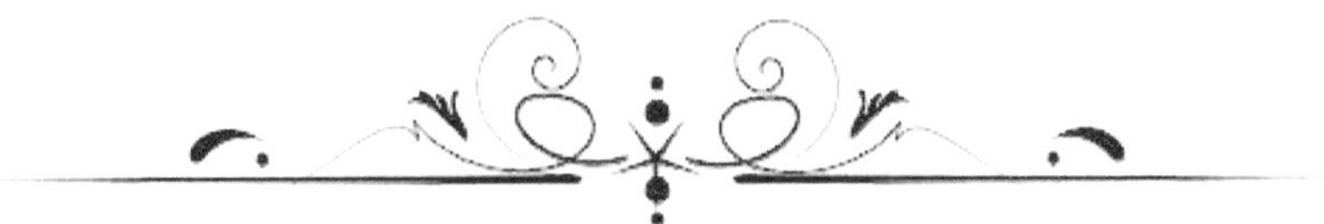

"If you want to lift yourself up, lift up someone else."

– Booker T. Washington

34

"You miss 100% of the shots you don't take."

– Wayne Gretzky

35

"It is never too late to be what you might have been."

– George Eliot

36

"A person who never made a mistake never tried anything new."

– Albert Einstein

37

"**The person who says it cannot be done should not interrupt the person who is doing it.**"

– Chinese Proverb

38

"Great minds discuss ideas;
average minds discuss
events; small minds discuss
people."

– *Eleanor Roosevelt*

39

"You only live once, but if you do it right, once is enough."

– Mae West

40

"If you tell the truth, you don't have to remember anything."

– *Mark Twain*

41

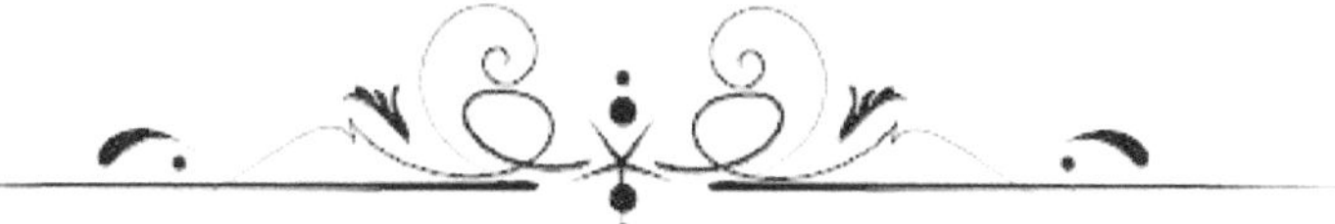

"The only thing worse than being blind is having sight but no vision."

– *Helen Keller*

42

"To live is the rarest thing in the world. Most people exist, that is all."

– Oscar Wilde

43

"Darkness cannot drive out darkness; only light can do that. Hate cannot drive out hate; only love can do that."

– Martin Luther King, Jr.

44

"The only thing we have to fear is fear itself."

– Franklin D. Roosevelt

45

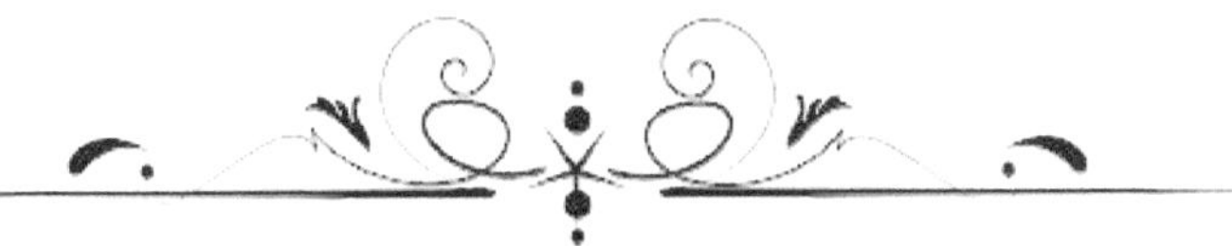

"If you look at what you have in life, you'll always have more. If you look at what you don't have in life, you'll never have enough."

– Oprah Winfrey

46

"**Remember no one can make you feel inferior without your consent.**"

– Eleanor Roosevelt

47

"For every minute you are angry you lose sixty seconds of happiness."

– *Ralph Waldo Emerson*

48

"Being deeply loved by someone gives you strength, while loving someone deeply gives you courage."

– Lao Tzu

49

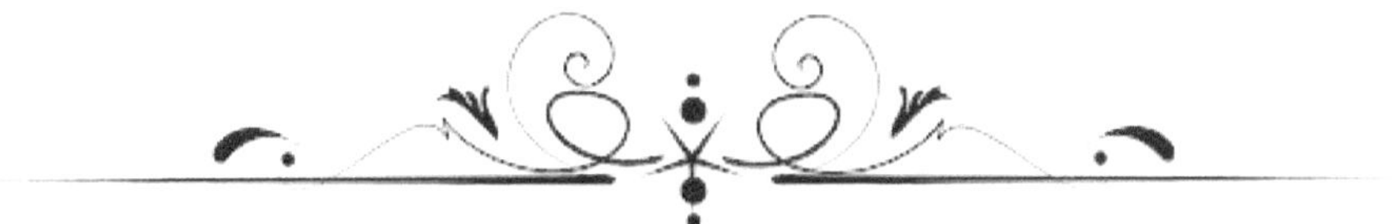

"There are two ways of spreading light: to be the candle or the mirror that reflects it."

– Edith Wharton

50

"The road to success and the road to failure are almost exactly the same."

– Colin R. Davis

51

"Motivation is a fire from within. If someone else tries to light that fire under you, chances are it will burn very briefly."

52

"In three words I can sum up everything I've learned about life: It goes on."

– Robert Frost

53

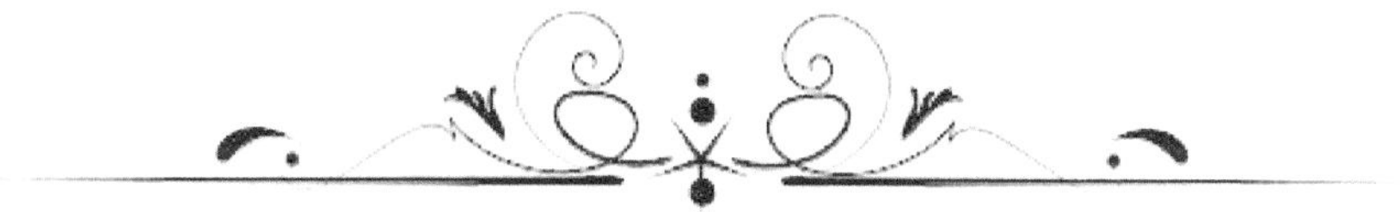

"Self-reverence, self-knowledge, self control — these three alone lead to power."

– Alfred, Lord Tennyson

54

"Though no one can go back and make a brand new start, anyone can start from now and make a brand new ending."

– Carl Bard

55

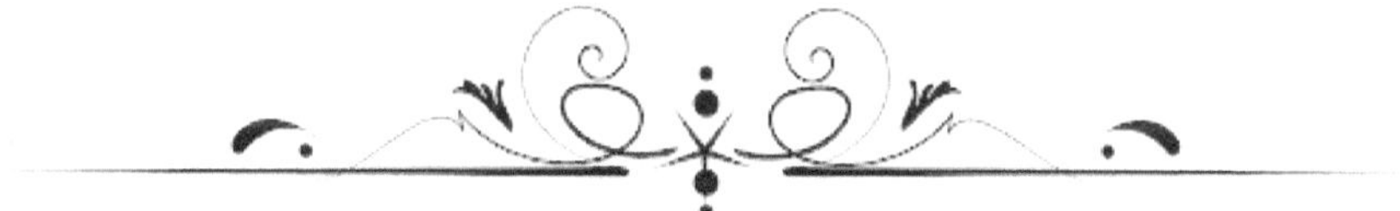

"A man who views the world the same at 50 as he did at 20 has wasted 30 years of his life."

– Muhammad Ali

56

"**Anyone who stops learning is old, whether at twenty or eighty. Anyone who keeps learning stays young. The greatest thing in life is to keep your mind young.**"

– Henry Ford

57

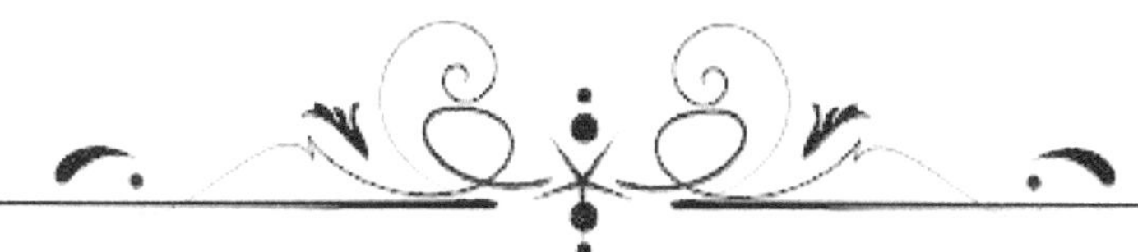

"He who angers you conquers you."

– Elizabeth Kenny

58

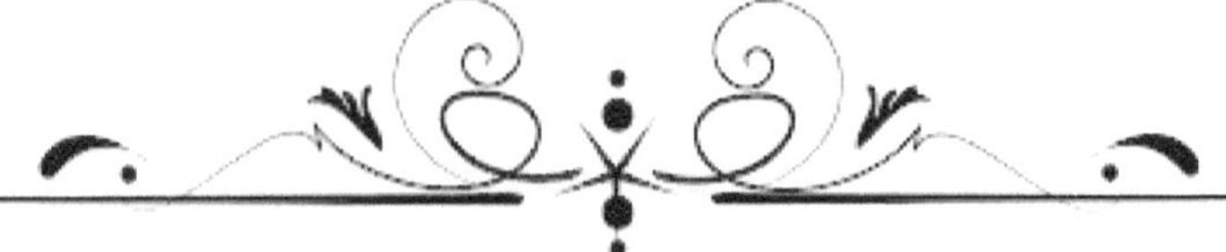

"Beauty, without expression, tires."

– Ralph Waldo Emerson

59

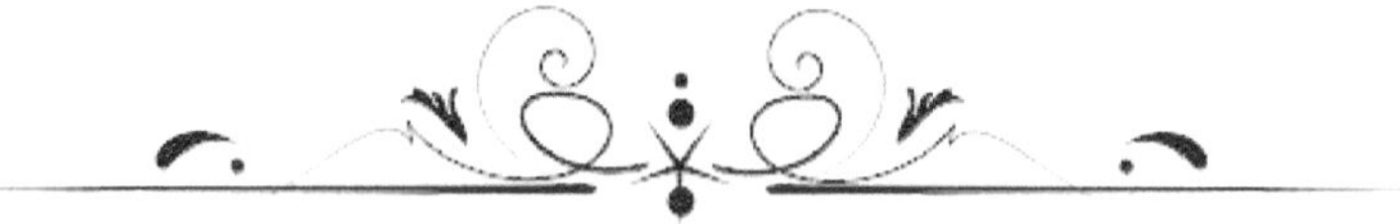

"The secret of business is to know something that nobody else knows."

– Aristotle Onassis

60

"The greatest discovery of all time is that a person can change his future by merely changing his attitude."

– Oprah Winfrey

61

"We cannot always build the future of our youth, but we can build our youth for the future."

– Franklin D. Roosevelt

62

"It takes courage to grow up and turn out to be who you really are."

– E.E. Cummings

63

"In this world nothing can be said to be certain, except death and taxes."

– Benjamin Franklin

64

"It is the mark of an educated mind to be able to entertain a thought without accepting it."

– Aristotle

65

"A happy family is but an earlier heaven."

– George Bernard Shaw

66

"Don't walk in front of me, I may not follow. Don't walk behind me, I may not lead. Walk beside me and be my friend."

– Albert Camus

67

"Courage doesn't always roar. Sometimes courage is the little voice at the end of the day that says 'I'll try again tomorrow.'"

– Mary Anne Radmacher

68

"Education is like a double-edged sword. It may be turned to dangerous uses if it is not properly handled."

– *Wu Ting-Fang*

69

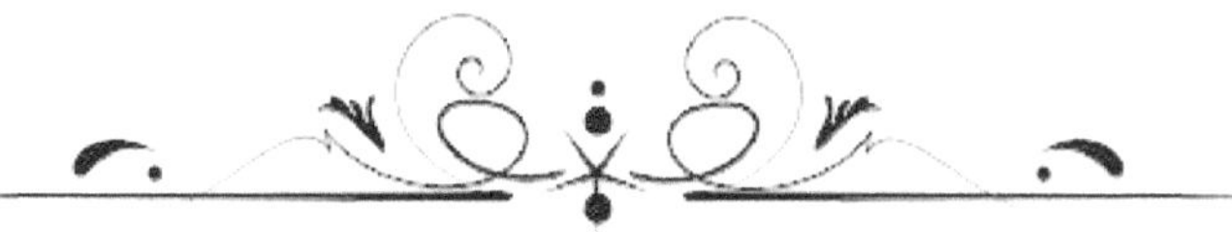

“Walking with a friend in
the dark is better than
walking alone in the light.”

– Helen Keller

"Happiness is not a goal; it is a by-product."

– Eleanor Roosevelt

71

"Always forgive your enemies; nothing annoys them so much."

– Oscar Wilde

72

"The only true wisdom is knowing that you know nothing."

– Socrates

73

"As a well-spent day brings happy sleep, so a life well spent brings happy death."

– Leonardo da Vinci

74

"Courage is what it takes to stand up and speak. Courage is also what it takes to sit down and listen."

– Winston Churchill

75

"Children are our most valuable resource."

– Herbert Hoover

76

"Love is, above all else, the gift of oneself."

– Jean Anouilh

77

“Music in the soul can be heard by the universe.”

– Lao Tzu

78

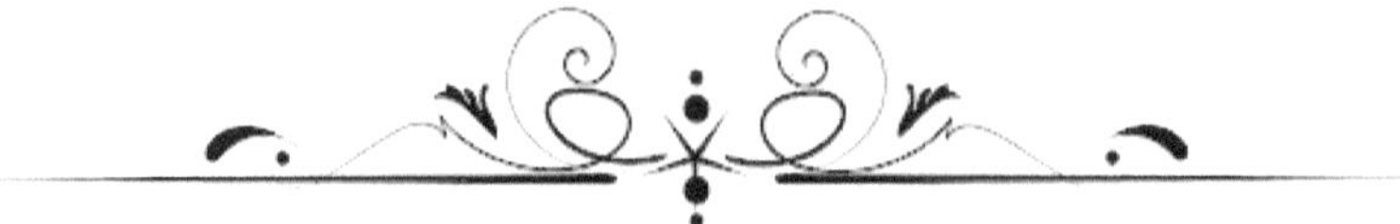

"Peace begins with a smile."

– Mother Teresa

79

"Success is liking yourself,
liking what you do, and
liking how you do it."

– Maya Angelou

80

> **"A friend is someone who knows all about you and still loves you."**
>
> *– Elbert Hubbard*

81

"Never leave that till tomorrow which you can do today."

– Benjamin Franklin

82

"If you don't make mistakes, you're not working on hard enough problems."

– Frank Wilczek

83

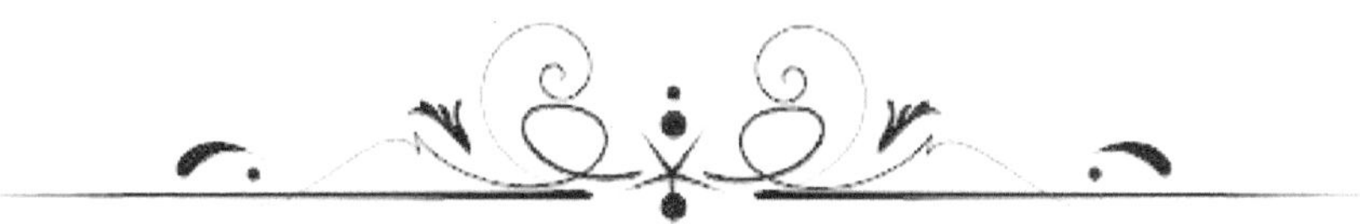

"We must learn to live together as brothers or perish together as fools."

– *Martin Luther King, Jr.*

84

"Life is like a camera. Just focus on what's important, capture the good times, develop from the negatives, and if things don't work out, just take another shot."

– Unknown

85

"When you judge another, you do not define them; you define yourself."

— Wayne Dyer

86

"Opportunity is missed by
most people because it is
dressed in overalls and
looks like work."

– Thomas Edison

87

"Love me when I least deserve it, because that's when I really need it."

– Swedish Proverb

88

"The best and most beautiful things in the world cannot be seen or even touched. They must be felt with the heart."

– Helen Keller

89

"If you want to test your memory, try to recall what you were worrying about one year ago today."

– E. Joseph Cossman

90

"The real opportunity for
success lies within the
person and not in the job."

– Zig Ziglar

91

"It takes a great deal of courage to stand up to your enemies, but even more to stand up to your friends."

– J. K. Rowling

92

"Defeat is not bitter unless you swallow it."

– Joe Clark

93

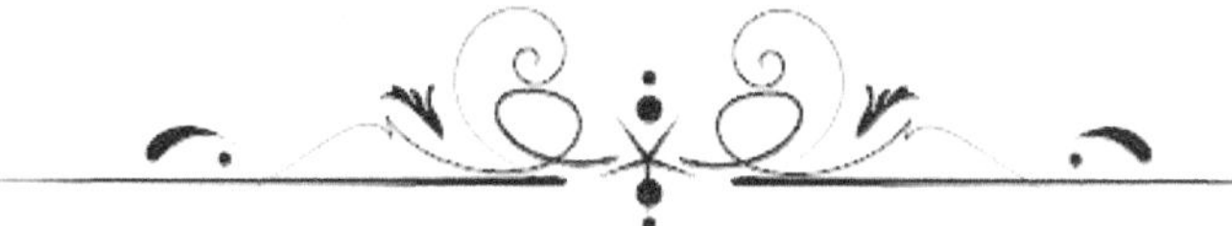

"A mind is like a parachute. It doesn't work if it isn't open."

– *Frank Zappa*

94

"The man who removes a mountain begins by carrying away small stones."

– Chinese Proverbs

95

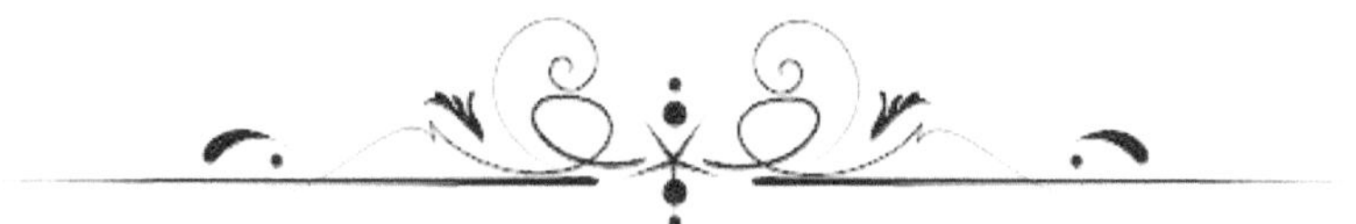

"When you are totally at peace with yourself, nothing can shake you."

– Deepam Chatterjee

96

"Be a first rate version of yourself, not a second rate version of someone else."

– Judy Garland

97

"Your worth consists in what you are and not in what you have."

– Thomas Edison

98

"Others can stop you temporarily – you are the only one who can do it permanently."

– Zig Ziglar

99

"Life has no limitations, except the ones you make."

– Les Brown

100

"Peace comes from within.
Do not seek it without."

– Muhammad Ali

101

"He who is not courageous enough to take risks will accomplish nothing in life."

– Muhammad Ali